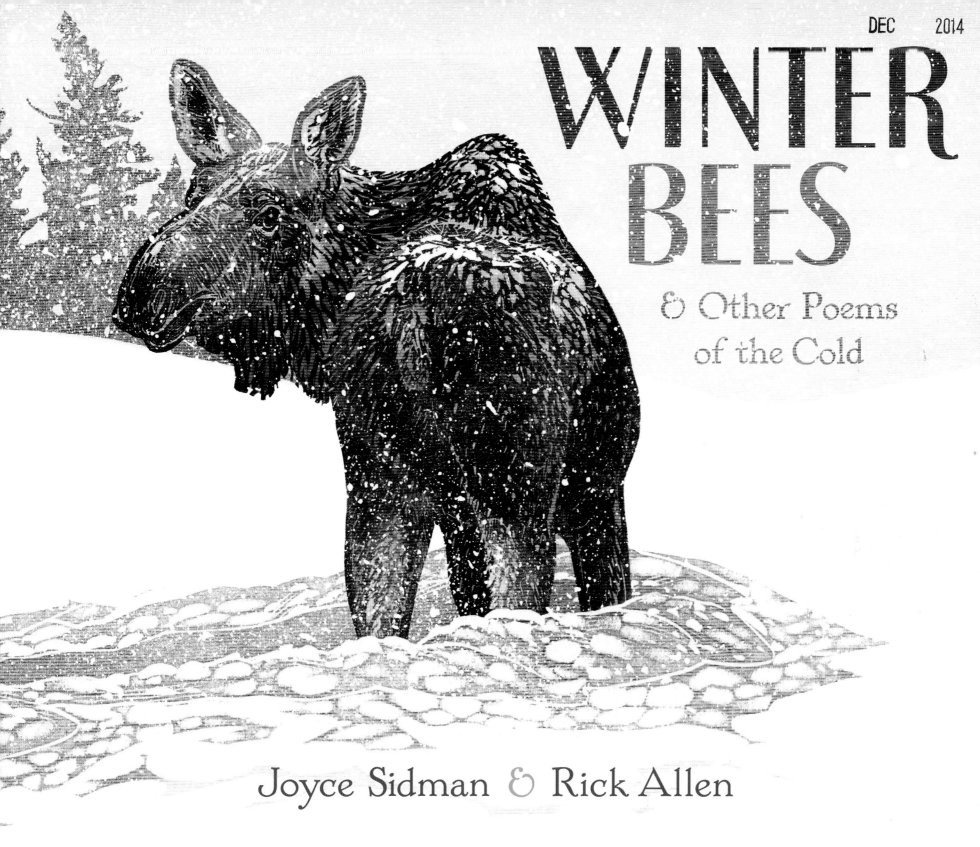

WINTER BEES

& Other Poems of the Cold

DEC 2014

Joyce Sidman & Rick Allen

Houghton Mifflin Harcourt

Boston   New York

For the wise wordsmiths: Laura, Mary, Michelle, Tracy & Tunie —J.S.

To Marian, for her two percent —R.N.A.

Library of Congress Cataloging-in-Publication Data
Sidman, Joyce.
[Poems. Selections]
Winter Bees & Other Poems of the Cold / Written by Joyce Sidman and illustrated by Rick Allen.
pages cm
Audience: Age: 6–10. Audience: Grade: K to Grade 4.
ISBN 978-0-547-90650-8
I. Allen, Rick, ill. II. Title. III. Title: Winter Bees and Other Poems of the Cold.
PS3569.I295A6 2014
811'.54—dc23
2013039007

Manufactured in China
SCP 10 9 8 7 6 5 4 3 2 1

4500480786

CONTENTS

Dream of the Tundra Swan

Dusk fell
and the cold came creeping,
came prickling into our hearts.
As we tucked beaks
into feathers and settled for sleep,
our wings knew.

That night, we dreamed the journey:
ice-blue sky and the yodel of flight,
the sun's pale wafer,
the crisp drink of clouds.
We dreamed ourselves so far aloft
that the earth curved beneath us
and nothing sang but
a whistling vee of light.

When we woke, we were covered with snow.
We rose in a billow of white.

Why do some birds migrate as winter approaches? Because the best spots for raising chicks are not always the best places to spend the winter. True to their name, **tundra swans** breed in the treeless tundra of far northern Canada and Alaska. Summer in these arctic regions—bathed in almost twenty-four-hour sunlight—is bountiful and lush. Swans feed and raise young on new shoots and aquatic plants. But when the weather turns cold, they move in huge flocks to "staging areas" along river deltas or marshes where the water is still free of ice. Here they rest and eat until the time is right for the 2,000-mile journey to warmer coastal areas such as New Jersey or California. During migration, tundra swans fly in V formations at up to 5,000 feet, and keep track of one another with a high, warbling call.

SNAKE'S LULLABY

Brother, sister, flick your tongue
and taste the flakes of autumn sun.

Use these last few hours of gold
to travel, travel toward the cold.

Before your coils grow stiff and dull,
your heartbeat slows to winter's lull,

seek the sink of sheltered stones
that safely cradle sleeping bones.

Brother, sister, find the ways
back to the deep and tranquil bays,

and 'round each other twist and fold
to weave a heavy cloak of cold.

Snakes, like other reptiles, are ectothermic ("outwardly heated") with no constant inner temperature. They bask in the sun to warm themselves, and in cold weather they become sluggish. Before autumn's warmth turns to winter, they must find a protected place to hibernate or they will freeze to death. Garter snakes often hibernate (or "brumate," as it is called in reptiles) in large groups, choosing underground tunnels, rocks, or caves below the frost line where the temperature is cool but not freezing. Most return to the same "hibernaculum" year after year, using their tongues to smell their way along age-old paths. In Manitoba, Canada, scientists have discovered hibernaculums that host up to 20,000 garter snakes! While brumating, snakes neither eat nor drink. Their breathing and heart rate slow down and their blood thickens. They spend the winter in a communal mass of motionless bodies, waiting for warmth.

Snowflake Wakes

Snowflake wakes,
whirling,
arms outstretched,
lace sprouting from fingertips

Leaps, laughing
in a dizzy cloud,
a pinwheel gathering glitter

Drops into air,
suddenly soft
and full, a lattice
of stars spinning
silently

Drifts down,
touching
and tickling,
clinging
and clumping

Hugs earth,
sighs and settles
Sleeps,
tucked in its own blanket

Snowflakes begin in clouds, where tiny water droplets freeze into ice. If the air is cold enough and there is plenty of moisture, bits of crystal form, which are six-sided because of the shape of the molecules that make up water itself. As these crystals swirl in the cloud, more and more water vapor freezes onto their surface and they begin to grow, gathering ice on each of their six points. Every snow crystal is slightly different because each follows a random path through the air as it grows. When the crystals are heavy enough, they drop from the cloud and fall, colliding and clinging to other crystals to form the snowflakes we see. Once snowflakes touch the ground, their delicate lace begins to break down and form a more solid layer of snow.

Big Brown Moose

I'm a big brown moose,
I'm a rascally moose,
I'm a moose with a tough, shaggy hide;
and I kick and I prance
in a long-legged dance
with my moose-mama close by my side.

I shrug off the cold
and I sneeze at the wind
and I swivel my ears in the snow;
and I tramp and I tromp
over forest and swamp,
'cause there's nowhere a moose cannot go.

I'm a big brown moose,
I'm a ravenous moose
as I hunt for the willow and yew;
with a snort and a crunch,
I rip off each bunch,
and I chew and I chew and I chew.

When together we slump
in a comfortable clump—
my mountainous mama and I—
I give her a nuzzle
of velvety muzzle.
Our frosty breath drifts to the sky.

I'm a big brown moose,
I'm a slumberous moose,
I'm a moose with a warm, snuggly hide;
and I bask in the moon
as the coyotes croon,
with my moose-mama close by my side.

Moose are built for cold. As the largest members of the deer family, they have huge bodies that trap heat well, and their fur is dense and warm. Their stiltlike legs wade through deep snowdrifts and snow-covered brush with ease, and broad cloven hooves steady them in icy terrain. Winter's main challenge for moose is to find enough plant material to power their enormous bulk; they are constantly on the lookout for food. Moose cows give birth in spring to a single calf (or occasionally twins), and the calf's survival depends fully on the mother's ability to teach it the ways of the woods. Moose cow and calf are rarely apart; they shelter together, evade wolves, and use their large, sensitive noses to seek out stands of nutritious willow and poplar twigs. They remain inseparable until the following spring, when the yearling calf must leave to make way for another newborn.

13

Winter Bees

We are an ancient tribe,
a hardy scrum.
Born with eyelash legs
and tinsel wings,
we are nothing on our own.
Together, we are One.

We scaled a million blooms
to reap the summer's glow.
Now, in the merciless cold,
we share each morsel of heat,
each honeyed crumb.
We cram to a sizzling ball
to warm our queen, our heart, our home.

Alone, we would falter and drop,
a dot on the canvas of snow.
Together, we boil, we teem, we hum.

Deep in the winter hive,
we burn like a golden sun.

Honeybees hang together at all times, but especially in winter. They are one of the few insects in the Northern Hemisphere that remain active in freezing weather, and they do it in typical bee fashion: by gathering, sharing, and communicating. All summer they collect nectar, which they transform into honey in wax-covered cells. As the air turns colder, bees begin to cluster around their queen, who represents the future of the hive. The colder it gets, the tighter they huddle, shrinking to a football-size mass that slowly eats its way through the carefully stored honey. Hungry hive-mates farther from the honeycomb will "beg" for food, which is then passed from bee to bee. When hive temperatures drop to dangerous levels, the outer-rim bees sound the alarm and the cluster begins to "shiver"—flex their flight muscles—to generate heat. While worker bees cycle in and out of the cluster's warm center, the queen remains at its heart, ready to resume her egg-laying at the first sign of spring.

Under Ice

(a pantoum)

In the fat white wigwam
made of ripped chips and thrashing twigs
is a heart of fur, curled and cozy,
far beneath the winter sunshine.

Made of ripped chips and thrashing twigs,
it gathers silence now
beneath the winter sunshine,
under ice, under snow.

It gathers silence now,
but in the dim oval room
under ice, under snow,
strong brown bullets dive.

16

In the dim oval room
they groom, snack, kiss:
strong brown bullets that dive
in the under-ice world.

They groom, snack, kiss:
a heart of fur, curled and cozy
in the under-ice world
of the fat white wigwam.

From the time their pond freezes over in autumn until it thaws in spring, **beavers** in northern climates do not once poke their heads out to see the sky. They remain active—diving in and out of the water, foraging for food, and grooming—but amazingly, they do it all *under the ice*. In late summer, beavers build a huge lodge made of mud and sticks that has snug rooms inside above the water line. The lodge's entrances are all underwater, but beavers are superb swimmers with dense fur that keeps their skin dry and warm. In fall, they stockpile a collection of juicy twigs in the water near the lodge. After the pond freezes over, they can dive beneath the ice, swim to their stockpile, grab a branch, and haul it back inside the lodge to munch. There is not much light—or room—inside the lodge for a family of up to six beavers, but they live quietly and harmoniously until spring's thaw.

BROTHER RAVEN, SISTER WOLF

You are Squawker, Croaker,
Alarm-on-the-wind.

You are Slinker, Shadow,
Nose-to-the-ground.

Fearful and flighty,
you peck and then flee.

Bound to the earth,
you leap, snap, and tumble.

Silver-winged Thief,

Yellow-eyed Snarler,

Stop following me!
Stop following me!

18

But don't stray too far.
Keep watching our woods.

Don't slack off your work.
Keep tracking our dinner.

Eyes-of-the-forest.

Heart-of-a-hunter.

Raven, my Brother.

My Sister, Wolf.

In northern regions, the lives of **wolves** and **ravens** are intertwined. While they do not exactly cooperate, each aids the other in the search for food. Ravens—intelligent, curious, and communicative—patrol from the sky and are quick to announce the presence of potential prey. Wolves—courageous, tireless, and expert trackers—work on the ground, hunting and bringing down deer, moose, elk, and smaller mammals. Wolves are drawn to the excited "discovery" cries of ravens, and ravens follow wolf packs, hoping for a meal. Once a kill is made, they feed together, though not always in harmony. They squabble, hoard food—even tease each other. Ravens have been observed sneaking up on a sleeping or distracted wolf, pecking its tail, and then dodging away as the wolf snaps in annoyance. Some scientists think ravens may pester resting wolves to keep them moving and hunting. Friend or foe, these two creatures share winter's challenge: finding enough food to survive the cold.

VOLE IN WINTER

Ambling through the hoary crystals,
thinking of how I love
this powdery place
between iron-hard ground
     and snow-crust ceiling . . .
how it bakes in the winter sun
like a crumbly white cake
studded with delectables:
crunchy roots, savory seeds,
     and tender bark of trees . . .
How it appeared so softly one night,
just as the bitter wind had almost
     sucked the very life from my bones:
a blanket made of sky-feathers!
Thinking of all the long, lovely tunnels
that smell of food, or sleep, or sky . . .
the way they twist and dive
in search of their own ends.
Thinking of—*Eeek!*

For small mammals like the **vole**, a thick blanket of snow in winter can mean the difference between life and death. Snow insulates the ground, keeping it much warmer than the air outside, and the snow layer nearest the earth crystallizes and turns sugary and loose, making it easy for tunneling. Voles, shrews, and mice—even red squirrels—all use this space, called the subnivean zone. Within the cozy subnivean, these animals carry on a secret life, creating a network of burrows and food caches. The snow offers some protection from foxes, owls, and coyotes; however, these predators can use their acute hearing to detect hidden movements, then pounce and dig down to capture prey. As snow melts in spring, subnivean creatures leave behind evidence of their winter lives: squiggles of small tunnels and nests in the grass.

Fox!

Stop thinking.

Run!

WHAT DO THE TREES KNOW?

What do the trees know?

>To bend when all the wild winds blow.

>Roots are deep and time is slow.

>All we grasp we must let go.

22

Trees, the giants of the plant world, survive winter in two very different ways. Coniferous (evergreen) trees have thin, wax-covered needles that tolerate freezing temperatures and remain on the tree all year round. Deciduous (leafy) trees, on the other hand, sprout large, flat leaves every spring that are perfect for gathering sunlight to produce energy. Deciduous trees grow like mad while the weather is warm, but in winter they essentially shut down. They shed their luxuriant leaves, which would freeze anyway and suck much-needed water from the tree. The tiny buds, which will hold next year's leaves, develop a tough, scaly coating to protect them all winter. As the temperatures drop, the living tissue in the tree's trunk undergoes a process called hardening, in which cells lose water and become more resistant to freezing. An early cold snap—before a tree has hardened—will damage its branches. But after hardening, the tree will spend the winter months dry, cold, and protected—waiting for spring to swell those hardy buds.

What do the trees know?

> Buds can weather ice and snow.
> Dark gives way to sunlight's glow.
> Strength and stillness help us grow.

CHICKADEE'S SONG

From dawn to dusk in darkling air
we glean and gulp and pluck and snare,
then find a roost that's snug and tight
to brave the long and frozen night.

We fluff and preen each downy feather,
Sing *fee-bee*—and laugh at the weather!
For if we're quick and bold and clever,
     winter's chill won't last forever.

The sun wheels high, the cardinal trills.
We sip the drips of icicles.
The buds are thick, the snow is slack.
Spring has broken winter's back.

24

Quick and bold and brave and clever,
we preen and fluff each downy feather.
Sing *fee-bee*—laugh at the weather—
     for winter doesn't last forever!

How does the tiny **chickadee**, weighing less than a handful of paperclips, stay alive in the bitter northern winter? By spending every waking moment searching for food. From just before dawn until the last light of dusk, chickadees hunt for seeds, berries, and hidden insects to build up a thin layer of fat, which must last them all night. Their dense feathers—which are not very aerodynamic, but perfect for short-distance swoops—help keep them warm. Chickadees find tiny roost-holes in trees or dense shrubs to conserve heat at night. They can even lower their body temperature to burn less fat. Sometimes a chickadee will hide a seed in a nighttime roost-hole for a much-needed snack upon waking. In late winter, chickadees sense the lengthening days and begin singing their *fee-bee* song, announcing a new nesting season.

The Whole World Is Melting

The whole world is melting!
The snow is slumping and dripping
and staining the bark black!
Roots poke from puddles,
and the leaf-litter where we live
is squishy-damp
      instead of frozen-hard,
and we have to move!
         We have to spring!
A mob of us, a mass of us, a throng of us
launching ourselves to the top
of the slippery snow,
      swarming its peaks and valleys!
And what will we find?
New moss, all ripe for slithering?
New loam, new love?

The whole world is melting
      and we are the first to see it,
wide awake on this lush winter day
as the trees grow wet and dark
and the earth warms and softens.
We are the first, the first!
We spring!

Spring!

Spring!

On warm winter days when the sun is strong, tiny creatures called **springtails**—or "snow fleas"—swarm up through layers of snow to congregate on bare patches of ground or the snow itself. About the size of this "s," these sturdy, wingless creatures are neither true fleas (they don't bite) nor true insects (their bodies have fewer segments). They belong to a class of arthropods called Collembola, and are very abundant in moist places—up to 6,000 springtails in a square foot of soil!—feeding on leaf mold and fungi. There are many types of springtails, but those that emerge in winter have special antifreeze in their bodies that allows them to frolic in the snow, looking for new places to eat and reproduce. Although they cannot fly, they have an explosive way of moving: they fold a tail-like spike (called a furcula) toward their abdomen and lock it with a tiny hook. When they want to move, their abdominal muscles release the hook, which drives the spike downward and flips them up into the air. Unfortunately they can't control where they land, but a flip or two is usually enough to get them out of danger, or into new munching grounds.

TRIOLET FOR SKUNK CABBAGE

Skunk cabbage peeks up through the snow:
  the first flower in the wood.
Wreathed in an eerie purple glow,
up through the slick of soggy snow,
smelling of rotten buffalo,
  it rears its speckled hood.
Skunk cabbage peeks up through the snow,
  the first flower in the wood.

In late wInter, a curiously odd flower appears in wet woodlands. The fist-size bud of the **skunk cabbage** burns up through the surrounding snow, using heat from special chemicals within its leaves. The purple hood pops open and lets out a powerful stink, much like rotting meat (or skunk scent). This potent smell attracts any flying insects that might be active. They swarm to the fleshy cluster of flowers within, looking for food and warmth—and pollinating it in the process. Thus the lowly skunk cabbage attracts spring's first pollinators, and gets a jump on other, sweeter-smelling and more beautiful flowers in the race to reproduce.

29

GLOSSARY

abdomen in insects, the hindmost (and usually the largest) part of the body.

aerodynamic sleekly designed to offer the least wind resistance.

aquatic living in the water.

arthropods a group of animals with a segmented body and an exoskeleton (skeleton on the outside of the body). Insects, spiders, scorpions, crabs, and centipedes are all arthropods.

brumate in reptiles, to go into a motionless state during cold weather, in which the body's functions slow down. Similar to hibernation in mammals.

cache a hiding place to store food or provisions.

Collembola a class of arthropods that live in soil.

coniferous a group of trees that have cones and keep their needlelike leaves through the winter.

deciduous a group of trees that shed their wide, flat leaves and stop all growth in winter.

ectothermic having a body temperature that varies with the environment; cold-blooded. Opposite is *endothermic,* or warm-blooded.

frost line the depth to which the soil freezes in the winter. Below this line soil is cold but not frozen.

furcula the tiny movable spike that springtails use to fling themselves into the air.

hardening the gradual process of chemical change and drying-out in the cells of plants that prepare them for winter's freezing temperatures.

hibernaculum a protected spot where mammals or reptiles go to hibernate.

hibernate in mammals, to go into a motionless, sleeplike state during cold weather, in which body temperature drops and breathing slows.

lattice a pattern of criss-crossed lines.

migration in birds, the seasonal journey from one region to another, in order to find food and raise young more successfully.

pantoum a poem form ("Under Ice") in which the second and fourth lines of a stanza are repeated as the first and third lines of the next stanza. In the final stanza, the first and third lines of the poem appear in reverse order, so that the last line of the poem is the same as the first.

pollinator an insect or other animal that carries pollen from one flower to another, fertilizing plants and allowing seeds to form.

subnivean literally "below [*sub*] the snow [*nivean*]." The area between the top layer of snow and the frozen ground.

triolet a poem form ("Triolet for Skunk Cabbage") with eight lines and a strict rhyme scheme. The first two lines are repeated as the last two, and the first line also recurs as the fourth.

vole a small rodent similar to a mouse, but with a thicker body and shorter tail.